ABOUT THE AUTHOR

Neil Ardley has written a number of innovative nonfiction books for children, including *The Eyewitness Guide to Music*. He also worked closely with David Macaulay on *The Way Things Work*. In addition to being a well-known author in the fields of science, technology, and music, he is an accomplished musician who composes and performs both jazz and electronic music. He lives in Derbyshire, England, with his wife and daughter.

Project Editor Phil Wilkinson
Art Editor Peter Bailey
Photography Pete Gardner
Additional photography Dave King
Created by Dorling Kindersley Limited, London

Library of Congress Cataloging-in-Publication Data
Ardley, Neil.
The science book of color/by Neil Ardley.
p. cm.
"Gulliver books."
Summary: Explains the principles of color and gives instructions for a variety of simple experiments.
ISBN 0-15-200576-5
1. Color—Juvenile literature. 2. Color—Experiments—Juvenile literature. [1. Color—Experiments. 2. Science—Experiments. 3. Experiments.] I. Title.
QC495.5.A73 1991
535.6—dc20 90-37166

Printed in Belgium by Proost
First U.S. edition 1991
A B C D E

THE SCIENCE BOOK OF COLOR

Neil Ardley

Gulliver Books

Harcourt Brace Jovanovich, Publishers

San Diego   New York   London

What is color ?

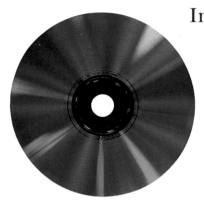

CD rainbow
The surface of a compact disc reflects many colors so we see a rainbow.

Imagine a world without color. It would be like living in an old movie. Color makes our world a pleasure to look at. All light rays contain color–the white light from the sun actually contains all the colors of the rainbow. When light shines on an object, only some colors bounce off it. Our eyes detect the colors in the light coming from objects and we see them as that particular color. Grass looks green, for example, because green light reflects off it. Red light bounces off a red rose.

Red for danger
Colors are often given meanings. Red usually means danger. Red and green mean stop and go in traffic signals.

Be seen at night
This safety harness is colored with a special dye that glows bright orange so that people can see it easily.

Finding a mate

Many birds display bright colors to attract other birds. The brilliant colors in a peacock's tail attract the peahen.

Mixing colors

When this wheel spins, the colored dots appear to merge and we see other colors. Television, photography, and printing create colored pictures by mixing just three basic colors.

⚠ This is a warning symbol. It appears within an experiment next to a step that requires caution. When you see this symbol, ask an adult for help.

Be a safe scientist
Follow all the instructions carefully and always use caution, especially with glass, scissors, matches, candles, and electricity. Never put anything into your mouth or eyes. Pour out water and colored liquids when you finish, and switch off flashlights and electric lights when you are done with them. Never touch the light bulbs—they get very hot.

Make a rainbow

Why do rainbows appear in the sky? Find out by turning white light from a flashlight into all the colors of the rainbow.

You will need:

Modeling clay    Flashlight

Mirror    Water   Shallow dish   White paper

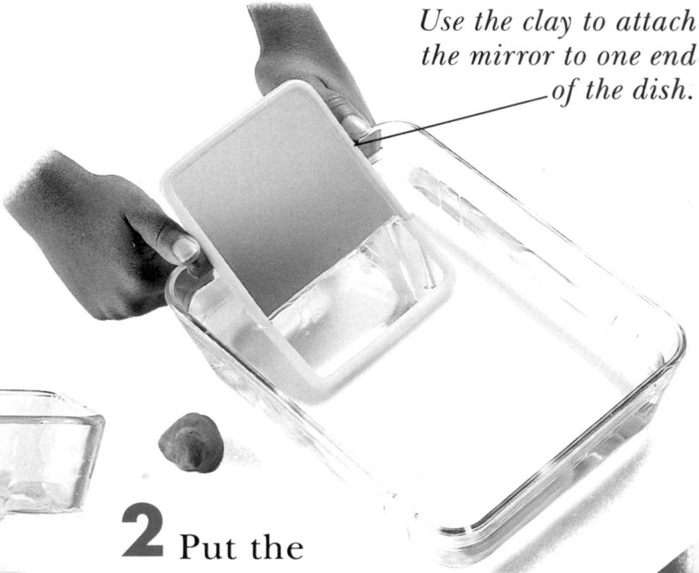

Use the clay to attach the mirror to one end of the dish.

1 Half fill the dish with water.

2 Put the mirror in the dish so it slants back against the side.

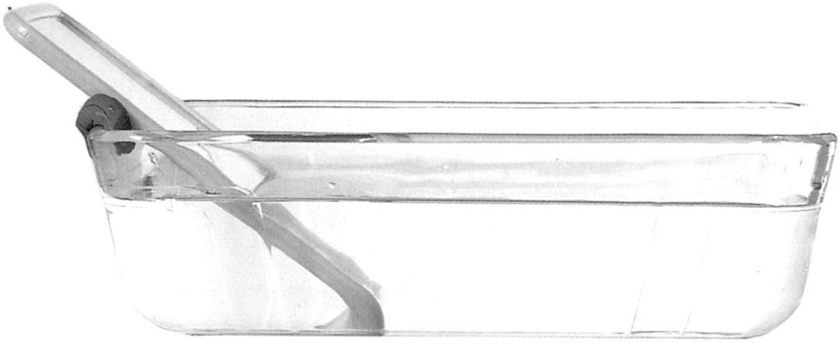

3 Shine the flashlight on the part of the mirror under the water.

4 Hold the piece of white paper above the flashlight. A rainbow appears on the paper.

Moving or tilting the flashlight may help you see the rainbow.

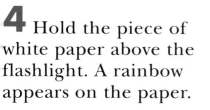

Curve of colors

When the sun shines through rain, the raindrops split the sun's white light into different colors. This forms a rainbow. The same thing happens with the flashlight and the water in the dish.

Sunset

The sky often looks orange or red when the sun sets. Find out why the sky changes color by making an orange and red sunset using a flashlight, milk, and water.

You will need:

Water   Milk

Flashlight

Spoon

White light from the flashlight

2 Add a little milk to the water.

1 Shine the flashlight through the water onto a white wall. It gives off a white light.

3 Stir the milky water with the spoon.

The milky water stops some colors in the light from getting through.

Only orange and red light rays pass through the milky water to reach the wall.

4 Now shine the flashlight through the white milky water. The wall lights up with an orange-red color!

Red sky at night
White light from the sun passes through the air. At sunset, only orange and red rays get through the air. Tiny particles of dust or smoke in the air stop all the other colors. The sun looks orange-red and it lights up the clouds with an orange-red color.

Colors from nowhere

Some sunglasses do more than reduce the sun's glare. They cut out some of the colors in white light, allowing others to reach the eyes. By making bright colors appear in clear plastic, you will see how this works.

You will need:

Polarizing sunglasses

Plastic cassette box

Lamp

1 Place the opened cassette box on a table and aim the lamp to light the box. Turn on the lamp.

2 Look at the box through the sunglasses.

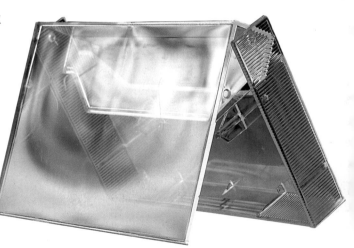

3 Bright colors appear in the plastic!

Breaking point
Polarized colors in a clear plastic disk are used by scientists to show stresses and strains in the disk.

Color box

Why does a red object look red? When light rays hit a surface, some are absorbed, others bounce off. The rays that bounce off determine the object's color.

You will need:

Tape

Red piece of cloth

White paper

Flashlight

Cardboard box

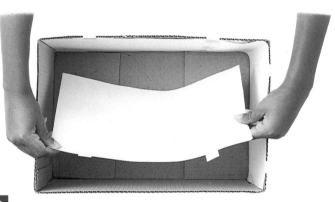

1 Fasten the white paper to the inner sides of the box.

2 Spread out the cloth to cover the bottom of the box.

3 Shine the flashlight on the cloth. The sides of the box turn deep red. You can try using pieces of cloth in other colors.

Red light bouncing off the surface of the cloth lights up the sides of the box.

Colored lights and shadows

You can light up your hand in different colors and make colored shadows appear. Do this by using pieces of colored plastic to change ordinary lamps into colored ones. You will see how light can change color.

You will need:

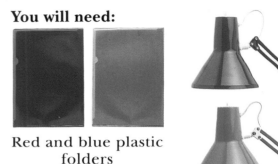

Red and blue plastic folders

Scissors   Tape   Two lamps

Make sure that the lamps are not plugged in.

1 Use the lamp shade to mark a circle on each folder.

2 Carefully cut out the circles.

The bulb must not touch the plastic.

3 ⚠ Tape the circles to the lamps. Ask an adult to plug in one lamp and turn it on.

4 Shine the lamp on a white surface. Its red light makes your hand look red with a dark shadow.

5 Build up a pattern with more strips. All kinds of different colors form just by using red, blue, and yellow.

Yellow and blue make green.

Yellow and red make orange.

Where the same colors overlap, a stronger version of the same color appears.

Blue and red make purple.

Red

Yellow

Blue

Black

Four inks combined

How many colors? Pictures in books contain three colored inks plus a black ink.

Circle of color

You can fool your eyes into seeing many different colors when in fact only red, green, and blue light comes to your eyes. This is what happens when you watch color television.

You will need:

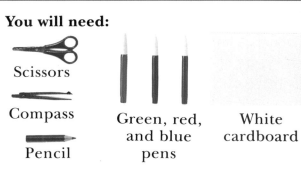

Scissors

Compass

Pencil

Green, red, and blue pens

White cardboard

1 Use the compass to draw a circle on the cardboard.

2 Carefully cut out the cardboard circle.

3 Use the three colored pens to draw red, green, and blue dots on the circle.

4 Push the pencil through the center of the circle.

The red, green, and blue dots appear to spread out and form rings.

Light from the colors in the dots makes a ring and mixes together. Red and green light combine to create a yellowish color.

5 Spin the circle like a top. Rings of different colors appear!

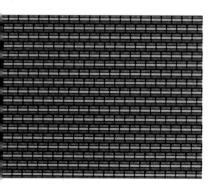

Patchwork picture

Examine a color television set with a magnifying glass. The picture is made of tiny patches that light up in red, green, and blue. The patches merge together when you look at the screen from a distance. The three colors of light mix together to create all the colors in the picture.

Hidden colors

Some colors are not what they seem. You can show that they are made of lots of different colors mixed together. It's easy to find the hidden colors in the inks in felt-tipped pens.

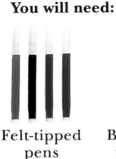

Felt-tipped pens

Blotting paper

Bowl of water

Clothespins

String

Scissors

Coffee filters also work.

1 Cut the blotting paper into strips.

2 Draw a circle of a different color near the bottom of each strip.

3 Tie the string to some supports to keep it in place above the bowl. Attach the strips of paper to the string. Arrange them so that the water touches the bottom edges but does not reach the ink.

Leave a space between the water and the ink.

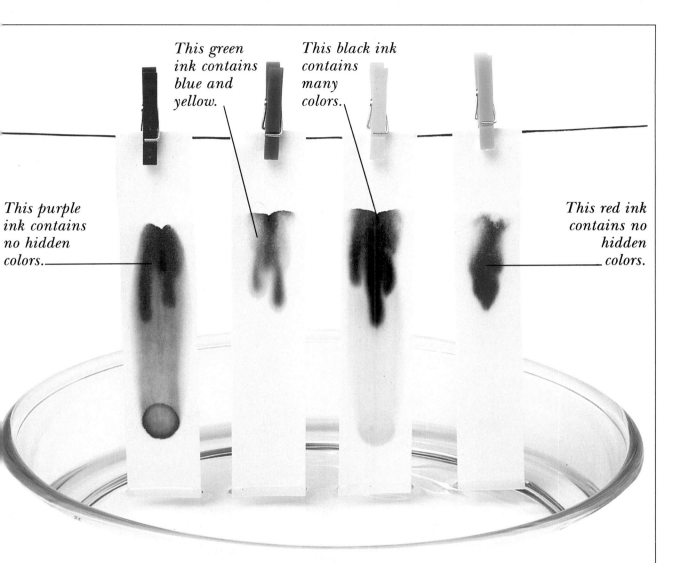

This green ink contains blue and yellow.

This black ink contains many colors.

This purple ink contains no hidden colors.

This red ink contains no hidden colors.

4 The water moves up the paper. Colors move different distances with the water, and each ink may separate into several colors.

Making paints

Paints come in many different shades of color, but in fact they contain hidden colors. Paints are made by mixing pigments of several basic colors together in different amounts. Artists mix paints together in a similar way when they paint a picture.

Color test

Things can suddenly change color as if by magic. You can make some color changes, and use them as a test.

You will need:

Knife   Soap   Lemon

Two large jars   Three small jars   Funnel   Coffee filters   Chopped red cabbage

Use the funnel and coffee filter to strain the juice.

1 ⚠ Pour hot water into a container of chopped red cabbage. Let it sit for a few minutes.

2 Strain the cabbage juice and pour some into each small jar.

3 Add some lemon juice to one jar.

4 Add some soap to another jar and stir.

Lemon is an acid. It turns the juice red.

This jar contains only cabbage juice.

Soap is a base. It turns the juice green.

5 The color of the cabbage juice changes from its usual purple to other colors.

Compare the colors of the two jars with a jar containing nothing but cabbage juice.

Try adding other things. Acids turn the juice red, bases turn it green or blue.

Other things to try
Vinegar
Bicarbonate of soda
Baking powder
Grapefruit juice
Apple juice
Fizzy drinks

Living color test
Hydrangeas have blue flowers in acidic soil but pink flowers in alkaline soil. Adding an acid or base (alkali) to the soil can make hydrangea flowers change from one color to the other.

Invisible ink

You can send a secret message or code to a friend using invisible ink. A color change will allow your friend to see the message or code hidden on the paper.

You will need:

Brush

Dish

Lemon

Iodine solution

White paper   Eyedropper   Bottle

1 Squeeze the lemon juice into the dish.

2 ⚠ Put some water into the bottle. Ask an adult to add a few drops of iodine.

Store the iodine in a safe place.

3 With the lemon juice, write a secret message on the paper. Allow it to dry.

4 Brush the paper with the iodine and water mixture.

24

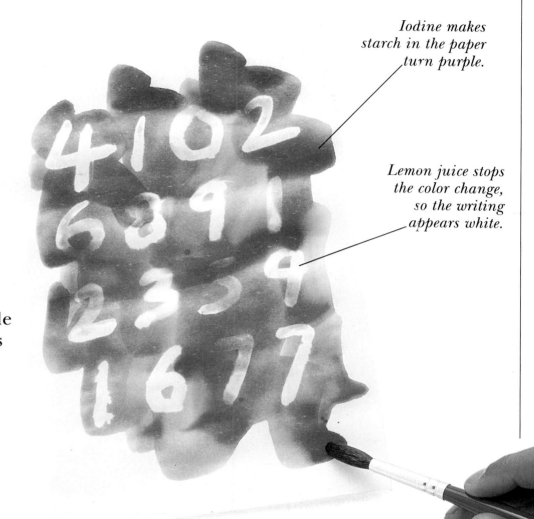

Iodine makes starch in the paper turn purple.

Lemon juice stops the color change, so the writing appears white.

5 The invisible writing appears on the paper!

Search for starch

Starch is a part of many foods. You can test foods for starch by adding a drop of iodine to them. It turns starchy foods deep purple. Try potatoes, bread, and rice. Throw away the food afterward.

Printing patterns

You can print brilliant colored patterns on paper by using oil, water, and paint. You will get a different pattern each time you try. You will also see how printing transfers colored inks to paper.

You will need:

Palette

Bowl of water

Brush

Linseed oil

Paper

Poster paints

Keep the colors separate.

1 Put some poster paints on the palette.

2 Add a little linseed oil to each color and stir well.

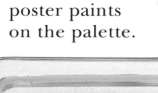

3 Dip your brush into one of the colors and touch it onto the water.

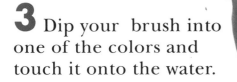

4 Do the same with other colors. Push or swirl the colors around to create a pattern.

5 Carefully lay a sheet of paper down on top of the pattern.

6 Gently peel the paper away from the surface of the water.

7 Leave the paper on a flat surface until it is dry. Print more patterns using different color combinations.

Red and blue

Red and yellow

Yellow and blue

Printing press
Some printing machines use a method similar to this experiment. An image is drawn on a printing plate in an oily material. The plate is then put in water. The ink only attaches itself to the oily areas, which repel the water.

Making colors

Use vegetables to make your own dyes. These homemade dyes create muted shades, unlike the strong colors of modern artificial dyes.

You will need:

Clean white cotton handkerchiefs

Saucepan

Rubber gloves

Large bowl

Beets

Strainer

Onion skins

1 ⚠ Put the onion skins in the saucepan and cover them with water. Ask an adult to boil them for 15 minutes. Then leave the pan to cool.

2 Pour the liquid through the strainer into the bowl.

Clear yellow dye

3 Put on the rubber gloves and dip the handkerchief into the liquid.

4 Squeeze out the handkerchief. Lay it on a clean sheet of paper to dry.

Handkerchief dyed with beet juice

Handkerchief dyed with onion skins

5 Repeat steps 1 to 4 with the beets. The colors may fade or wash out.

Powder paints

Long ago, people made paints by crushing colored rocks and mixing the powder with oil. This red comes from rocks containing the mineral cinnabar.

Picture credits
Picture credits abbreviation key:
B=below, C=center, L=left, R=right,
T=top)

Pete Gardner: 6BR, 7CL; The
Image Bank: 6CL, 9BL, 13BL; Colin
Keates: 29CL; ICI Paints: 21BL;
London Features International
Ltd./David Koppel: 15BL; Nimbus
Records: 6TL; Pershke Price

Service Organisation Ltd.: 27BL;
Science Photo Library/Peter
Aprahamian/Sharples Stress
Engineers Ltd: 10BL; Vaughan
Fleming: 19BL; Jerry Young: 7TR

Picture research Cynthia Hole

Title page photography Dave King

Dorling Kindersley would like to
thank Claire Gillard for editorial
assistance and Mark Regardsoe for
design assistance; Mrs Bradbury, the
staff and children of Allfarthing
Junior School, Wandsworth,
especially Joe Armstrong, Mark
Baker, Melanie Best, Damien
Francis, and Alice Watling.